Lucy's Advice

LITTLE SIMON
An imprint of Simon & Schuster Children's Publishing Division
1230 Avenue of the Americas New York, New York 10020
Copyright © 2003 United Feature Syndicate, Inc. All rights reserved. PEANUTS is a registered trademark of
United Feature Syndicate, Inc.
READY-TO-READ, LITTLE SIMON, and colophon are registered trademarks of Simon & Schuster.
Manufactured in the United States of America
First Edition
2 4 6 8 10 9 7 5 3 1
CIP data for this book is available from the Library of Congress.
Library Edition ISBN 0-689-85475-7
Paperback ISBN 0-689-85473-0

Lucy's Advice

Based on the comic strips
by Charles M. Schulz
Adapted by Nancy Krulik
Art adapted by Peter and Nick LoBianco

Ready-to-Read

Little Simon
New York   London   Toronto   Sydney   Singapore

Some people called Lucy
a know-it-all.
But Lucy didn't mind.
She *did* know a lot.
That is why she gave
advice to everyone else—
for only five cents.

Lucy's little brother, Linus,
always carried his blanket.
He sucked his thumb, too.
That made Lucy crazy.
"If you listened to me,
you would not need that
thumb and blanket," she told him.

But Linus would not give up
his blanket.
"Years from now, when your kind
is gone, thumbs and blankets
will still be around," Linus said.
Lucy had some advice for him.
POW!

Schroeder told Lucy about a
piano player who could not
hear his own music.
That made Schroeder sad.
"Do not think about it,"
Lucy told Schroeder.
Some cases were simple.

Even though Lucy knew a lot,
she had one tough case.
That case was Charlie Brown.
She could not help him.
Charlie Brown was too wishy-washy.
No advice could change that.

But that did not stop Charlie Brown
from coming to Lucy for advice.
"How do I know if the advice
you are going to give me will be
any good?" he asked.

"Any advice you get here is
  guaranteed to be right on target,"
  Lucy told him.
"All right," Charlie Brown said.
"I will take a chance."
  He gave Lucy five cents.
"Sit up straight," she said.
"You are slouching."

That was not what Charlie Brown
had in mind.
"I want people to say,
'That Charlie Brown is a great guy,'"
he told Lucy. "I want to be liked.
Do you understand?"

"Sure, I understand," Lucy told him.
"Here is my advice. Forget it!"
 She held out her hand.
"Five cents, please."

THE DOCTOR IS IN

Poor Charlie Brown.
He did not have many friends.
"I feel lonely a lot of the time,"
he told Lucy.
"Try taking dance lessons,"
Lucy said.

"What if no one will dance with me?"
Charlie Brown asked.
Lucy shrugged.
"Then you will be a lonely person
who knows how to dance," she said.
"Five cents, please."

The next day, Charlie Brown
came back again.
"I have been thinking about your case,"
Lucy told him.
"What you need is a dog."

That was good advice.
Except Charlie Brown
already *had* a dog.
Who do you think *I* am?
Snoopy wondered. Kermit the Frog?

A few days later, Linus found
Charlie Brown talking to a tree.
He brought Charlie Brown to see Lucy.

As soon as Lucy heard about this,
she took out a pencil and paper.
"I had better take notes,"
she said. "This case could
make me famous!"

"How can a tree eat a kite
  if it does not have any teeth?"
  Lucy asked Charlie Brown.
"And how can a tree swallow a kite
  if it does not have a stomach?"

"A tree has limbs," said Charlie Brown,
"but that does not make it a track star.
  A tree has a trunk, but does that
  make it an elephant? If it has bark,
  does that make it a dog?" Charlie Brown
  laughed loudly at his own jokes.

During the interview,
Lucy wrote on her pad that the patient
suddenly became hysterical.

Lucy tried to make Charlie Brown
tell her what really happened.
But Charlie Brown had a question
for her.
"Tell *me* a great truth," he said.

Lucy smiled. She could do that.
"When you are getting a drink
 of water in the dark,
 always rinse out the glass,"
 she said. "There might be a bug in it."
 She held out her hand.
"Five cents, please."

"Great truths are even more simple
than I thought," Charlie Brown said
as he handed Lucy a nickel.

Charlie Brown still looked sad.
"Everything seems hopeless," he said.
Lucy thought very hard.
There had to be some advice
she could give poor Charlie Brown.
There had to be some way
to make him happy.

"Go home and eat a jelly bread
sandwich folded over,"
she said finally.

Charlie Brown smiled.
He actually smiled!
Then he stood up
and began to walk away.
Lucy stopped him.
"Five cents, please," she said.

Lucy leaned back in her chair.
She *had* helped Charlie Brown!
Good old wishy-washy Charlie Brown.
"There are some cures you
can't learn in medical school,"
she told herself proudly.